Contents

Introduction 3

Unit 1: Teacher Resources
Newsletter 4
Border Page 5
Special Days in May 6
May Calendar 7
Calendar Activities. 8
Mother's Day Activity Master. 9
Memorial Day Activity Master 10

Unit 2: See the Sea
Teacher Information 11
Arts and Crafts 12
Kid's Kitchen 13
Poem and Book List 14
Bulletin Board 15
Centers
    Language Center 16
    Math Center 16
    Science Center 17
    Social Studies Center. 17
    Writing Center 18
    Literacy Center 18
    Art Center. 19
    Physical Development Skills Center . . . 19
Patterns and Activity Masters
    Crab Word Slide Activity Master 20
    Fishy Fish Parts Activity Master 21
    World Map Activity Master 22
    Oyster Pattern. 23
    What's the Size? Activity Master 24
    Sea Life Patterns 25

Unit 3: Celebrate Cinco de Mayo
Teacher Information 26
Arts and Crafts 27
Kid's Kitchen 28
Poem and Book List 29
Bulletin Board 30

Centers
    Language Center 31
    Math Center 31
    Science Center 32
    Social Studies Center. 32
    Writing Center 33
    Communication Center 33
    Game Center. 34
    Music Center 34
Patterns, Cards, Poster, and Activity Masters
    Symbols of Cinco de Mayo Cards 35
    Spanish Number Words Poster 36
    Add and Subtract in Spanish
        Activity Master. 37
    What Senses? Activity Master 38
    Mexican Flag Symbols Patterns. 39
    Cinco de Mayo Is Fun!
        Activity Master. 40

Unit 4: Rocky Fun
Teacher Information 41
Arts and Crafts 42
Kid's Kitchen 43
Song and Book List 44
Bulletin Board 45
Centers
    Language Center 46
    Math Center 46
    Science Center 47

    Social Studies Center 47
    Writing Center 48
    Communication Center 48
    Physical Development Skills Center . . . 49
    Art Center. 49
Pattern and Activity Masters
    Rhymes with *Rock* Activity Master 50
    Do an Experiment Activity Master 51
    I See a Rock! Activity Master 52
    Wish List Activity Master 53
    Stone Pattern. 54
    Design a Statue Activity Master 55

Unit 5: All About Frogs and Toads
Teacher Information 56
Arts and Crafts 57
Kid's Kitchen 58
Riddles and Book List 59
Bulletin Board 60
Centers
    Language Center 61
    Math Center 61
    Science Center 62
    Social Studies Center. 62
    Writing Center 63
    Literacy Center 63
    Physical Development Skills Center . . . 64
    Communication Center 64
Pattern, Cards, and Activity Masters
    Frog Head Pattern 65
    Toad Head Pattern. 66
    Frog Life Cycle Cards 67
    Hopping Toad Patterns. 68
    Frog and Toad Vowels Activity Master. . 69
    Frog or Toad? Activity Master. 70

Unit 6: Sizzling Summer
Teacher Information 71
Arts and Crafts 72
Kid's Kitchen 73
Song and Book List 74
Bulletin Board 75
Centers
    Language Center 76
    Math Center 76
    Science Center 77
    Social Studies Center. 77
    Writing Center 78
    Technology Center 78
    Literacy Center 79
    Communication Center 79
Cards and Activity Masters
    Hot or Cold? Activity Master. 80
    It's a Fair Summer Activity Master 81
    Sounds Like Summer Activity Master. . . 82
    Pick a Place Activity Master 83
    Word Play Activity Master 84
    July Fourth Cards. 85

Unit 7: Author Study— Arnold Lobel
Teacher Information 86
Literature Selection and Activities 87
Book List. 88
Patterns and Activity Master
    Bookmark Patterns 89
    Coat Pattern 90
    Stationery Activity Master 91

Center Icons Patterns 92

Student Awards Patterns 95

Student Award/Calendar Day Patterns 96

Introduction

This series of monthly activity books is designed to give first and second grade teachers a collection of hands-on activities and ideas for each month of the year. The activities are standards-based and reflect the philosophy that children have different styles of learning. The teacher can use these ideas to enhance the development of the core subjects of language, math, social studies, and science, as well as the social/emotional and physical growth of children. Moreover, the opportunity to promote reading skills is present throughout the series and should be incorporated whenever possible.

Organization and Features

Each book consists of seven units:

Unit 1 provides reproducible pages and information for the month in general.
- a newsletter outline to promote parent communication
- a blank thematic border page
- a list of special days in the month
- calendar ideas to promote special holidays
- a blank calendar grid that can also be used as an incentive chart

Units 2–6 include an array of activities for five **theme** topics. Each unit includes
- teacher information on the theme
- arts and crafts ideas
- a food activity
- poetry, language skills (songs, poems, raps, and chants), and books
- bulletin board ideas
- center activities correlated to specific learning standards (Language arts, math, science, social studies, and writing are included in each theme.)

Implement the activities in a way that best meets the needs of individual children.

Unit 7 focuses on a well-known **children's author**. The unit includes
- a biography of the author
- activities based on a literature selection
- a list of books by the author
- reproducible bookmarks

In addition, each book contains
- reproducible **icons** suitable to use as labels for centers in the classroom. The icons coordinate with the centers in the book. They may also be used with a work assignment chart to aid in assigning children to centers.
- reproducible **student awards**
- **calendar day pattern** with suggested activities

Research Base

Howard Gardner's theory of multiple intelligences, or learning styles, validates teaching thematically and using a variety of approaches to help children learn. Providing a variety of experiences will assure that each child has an opportunity to learn in a comfortable way.

Following are the learning styles identified by Howard Gardner.
- **Verbal/Linguistic** learners need opportunities to read, listen, write, learn new words, and tell stories.
- **Bodily/Kinesthetic** learners learn best through physical activities.
- **Musical** learners enjoy music activities.
- **Logical/Mathematical** learners need opportunities to problem solve, count, measure, and do patterning activities.
- **Visual/Spatial** learners need opportunities to paint, draw, sculpt, and create artworks.
- **Interpersonal** learners benefit from group discussions and group projects.
- **Intrapersonal** learners learn best in solitary activities, such as reading, writing in journals, and reflecting on information.
- **Naturalist** learners need opportunities to observe weather and nature and to take care of animals and plants.
- **Existential** learners can be fostered in the early years by asking children to think and respond, by discussions, and by writing.

Gardner, H. (1994). *Frames of mind.* New York: Basic Books.

May News

Teacher: _____ Date: _____

Headline News

Coming Up

Happy Birthday to

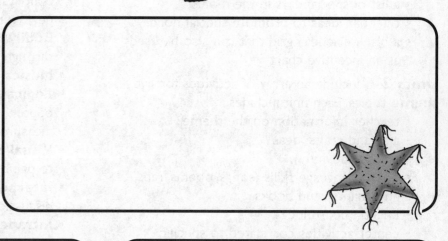

Special Thanks to

Help Wanted

Special Days in May

American Bike Month Challenge children to name the parts of a bicycle and have them describe their favorite place to ride their bike.

Mother's Day This special day falls on the second Sunday in May. Have children celebrate with the activity on page 9.

1 Mother Goose Day Invite children to choose and read aloud a favorite Mother Goose poem. Challenge children to find the rhyming words.

2 Brother/Sister Day Have children dictate or write a sentence telling something they like to do with their brother or sister. For children that have no siblings, have them write about a close friend or relative.

4 National Kids' Fitness Day Discuss with children the importance of exercise to stay fit and healthy. Encourage them to jog around the school playground or participate in several fitness exercises.

5 Cinco de Mayo Have children celebrate with activities from the Celebrate Cinco De Mayo unit that begins on page 26.

8 No Socks Day Invite children to wear shoes with no socks on this day.

10 Clean Up Your Room Day Pair children and assign partners one area of the room to clean.

11 Jigsaw Day Provide several age-appropriate jigsaw puzzles and have a puzzle competition. Have children work together in small groups to complete the puzzles.

15 International Day of Families Display pictures of families from other countries. Then invite children to draw a picture of their family and add it to the display.

16 First U.S. Nickel Minted (1866) Discuss with children that a nickel is a coin that is worth five cents. Have them use real coins to practice money skills.

17 First Kentucky Derby (1875) Invite children to bring a stick horse from home and have relay races.

19 Frog Jumping Jubilee Day Have children celebrate with activities from the All About Frogs and Toads unit that begins on page 56.

20 Strawberries Day Read *The Little Mouse, The Red Ripe Strawberry, and The Big Hungry Bear* by Don Wood and Audrey Wood (Child's Play International, Ltd.). Bring strawberries to class. Have children cut a strawberry in half and share it with a friend.

26 Sally Ride's Birthday (1951) Display a picture of Sally Ride and explain to children that she became the first woman astronaut in 1983. Invite them to draw a picture of her in the space shuttle.

31 Memorial Day Invite children to tell about someone that they know who is or was in the military. Then have them color a picture of the United States flag.

May

Sunday	Monday	Tuesday	Wednesday	Thursday	Friday	Saturday

Using the Calendar for Basic Instruction in the Classroom

The children you teach may enjoy using the calendar-related games and activities on this page to practice other skills.

Word Problems During daily calendar time, practice problem solving by asking children to use the calendar to answer a question. For example: It rained all week except on Monday, Wednesday, and Thursday. On which days did it rain? You may wish to relate the questions to holidays or units of study.

Graphing Make a line graph to hang on the wall. Write the numbers 1–6 on the vertical axis and the twelve months of the year on the horizontal axis. Find out how many children have a birthday in each month and record on the graph. Connect the points to finish the line graph. You may wish to have the children copy the data and make individual line graphs.

Patterning Give children a calendar page for any month that you choose. Decide on a specific color pattern, such as red, yellow, and green. Have children color three days in the middle of the calendar red, yellow, and green. Then, have them color all of the remaining days using the same pattern. They will be extending patterns forward and backward.

Distances on a Number Grid Give children a calendar page of your choice. Have them find how many spaces they move from one number to another number. Example: How many spaces do you move to go from 17 to 23?

Special Days Use the activity masters on pages 9 and 10 to expand children's knowledge of the calendar and special days. The information for these special days is included below.

Mother's Day is celebrated on the second Sunday in May. This day has its roots in the United States. Julia Ward Howe held Mother's Day meetings in Boston in 1872. Howe wanted people to reflect on peace after the emotional upheaval of the Civil War. Anna Reese Jarvis, trying to encourage a national holiday, furthered the efforts. In 1914, President Woodrow Wilson officially proclaimed the second Sunday in May as Mother's Day.

Memorial Day is a national holiday in the United States. The day honors soldiers who have died in all of America's wars. The day was first called Declaration Day and was observed on May 30, 1868, to honor those who had died during the Civil War. People decorated soldiers' graves with flags and flowers. Some places had parades and held ceremonies. Over the years, people began to recognize other soldiers who had died in an American war. In 1968, the last Monday in May was established as the official day to observe Memorial Day.

Great Rock Facts

 Rocks are made of one or more minerals. These minerals vary in color and texture.

 Rocks are constantly being changed by the environment. This is called the rock cycle.

 Rocks are classified according to how they are formed. There are three kinds of rock: igneous, sedimentary, and metamorphic.

 Igneous means made from fire or heat. When a volcano erupts, the magma or hot lava spills out on the surface and cools. The magma turns from a liquid to a solid to form igneous rocks.

 Sometimes the magma cools quickly and traps gas bubbles inside to form a rock called pumice. It is the only rock that floats.

 Sedimentary rocks are formed by layers of sediments from sand, mud, animal material, or plant material. Fossils of animals and plants are found in sedimentary rocks.

 Seventy percent of all rocks on the surface of the Earth are sedimentary.

 Metamorphic rocks are formed by adding heat and pressure to igneous or sedimentary rocks. The heat and pressure change the rock formation.

 Geodes are fascinating geological formations. A geode is a spherical lump with a hollow cavity filled with crystals.

 Rock crystals are transparent crystalline minerals that form a definite shape.

 A geologist is a scientist who studies the surface of the Earth and its layers.

Rock Paperweights

Materials

- medium rocks, 3–4 inches in size
- tempera paints
- paintbrushes
- bowls
- large paper plates
- newspaper

Directions

Teacher Preparation: Spread newspaper on a table and pour paints into the bowls. Put a paintbrush in each bowl.

1. Choose a rock and place it on a plate.
2. Paint the rock with a picture or a design.
3. Set the rock aside to dry.

Gee, It's a Geode!

Materials

- a geode
- pantyhose plastic eggs or small plastic eggs
- brown lunch bags
- iridescent glitter
- purple, gold, and silver glitter
- glue
- bowl
- scissors

Directions

Teacher Preparation: Display a geode and discuss how it is made. Cut the lunch bags along one side and cut off the bottom. If children will be using the smaller eggs, cut the bags into thirds.

1. Get a cut bag and crush it into a ball. Open it up and flatten it out.
2. Get half of a plastic egg and cover the inside with a layer of glue.
3. Wrap the paper bag around the outside of the egg to form the outside of the geode.
4. Push the edges of the bag inside the egg. The bag does not have to be smooth. The glue will hold the bag in place.
5. Spread glue inside the egg again so the paper inside the egg is totally covered.
6. Sprinkle glitter inside the egg. Shake the excess glitter into a bowl.
7. Set the geode aside to dry.

Metamorphic Rocks

You will need

- rice cereal
- ball-shaped cereal
- chocolate chips
- marshmallow cream
- spoons
- foil
- permanent marker
- paper plates
- electric skillet
- scissors

Directions

Teacher Preparation: Pour the cereals and the chips into bowls. Then cut the foil into squares. Heat the skillet to low and place the foil squares in the skillet once children combine the ingredients. Remove the foil squares from the skillet and place them on paper plates once the ingredients start to melt. Set them aside until cooled. Explain that metamorphic rocks are made when heat is added to sedimentary rocks.

1. Get a piece of foil and write your name along one edge.
2. Put a spoonful of marshmallow cream on the foil.
3. Put a spoonful of chocolate chips on the cream.
4. Put a spoonful of each cereal on the chips.
5. Give the foil square to an adult to put in the skillet. Watch what happens when heat is added.
6. Enjoy eating the metamorphic rocks when they are cool!

Note: Be aware of children who may have food allergies.

🎵 I Found a Rock

(Tune: "If You're Happy and You Know It")

Note: You may wish to display each kind of rock as children sing about it.

I found a rock that is igneous. (clap, clap)
I found a rock that is igneous. (clap, clap)
It came from a volcano
And was made by heat and fire.
I found a rock that is igneous. (clap, clap)

I found a rock that is sedimentary. (clap, clap)
I found a rock that is sedimentary. (clap, clap)
It has many, many layers
Of fossils, sand, and mud.
I found a rock that is sedimentary. (clap, clap)

I found a rock that is metamorphic. (clap, clap)
I found a rock that is metamorphic. (clap, clap)
It was changed by heat and pressure
And became a different kind.
I found a rock that is metamorphic. (clap, clap)

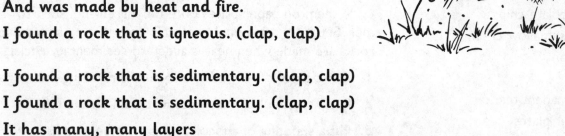

Rock and Read

The Best Book of Fossils, Rocks, and Minerals
by Chris Perrault
(Larousse Kingfisher Chambers)

Dave's Down to Earth Rock Shop
by Stuart J. Murphy (HarperCollins)

Everybody Needs a Rock
by Byrd Baylor (Scott Foresman)

Let's Go Rock Collecting
by Roma Gans (HarperCollins)

Looking at Rocks
by Jennifer Dussling (Grosset & Dunlap)

Rocks in His Head
by Carol Otis Hurst (Greenwillow)

Sculpture and Drama
by Vincent Douglas (Waterbird Press)

Stone Soup
by Ann McGovern (Scholastic)

Sylvester and the Magic Pebble
by William Steig (Aladdin Library)

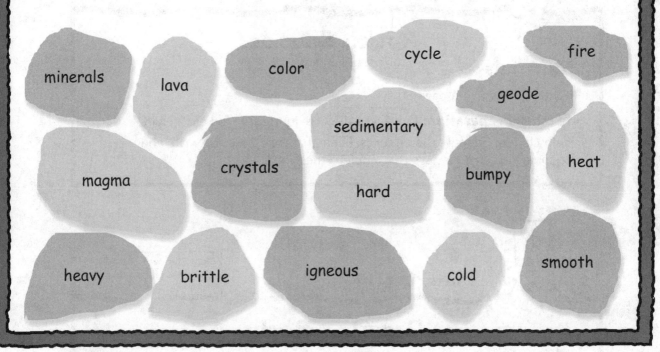

A Rocky Word Wall

Materials

- a variety of shades of brown and gray construction paper
- yellow craft paper
- border
- scissors
- markers
- stapler

Directions

Teacher Preparation: Cover the bulletin board in yellow paper. Add the caption and border. Invite children to make a word wall with words and phrases related to rocks. Once the wall is complete, review all the words in a final discussion about rocks.

1. Cut a rock shape out of construction paper.
2. Write a word or phrase that describes or names a rock.

Have children identify their word or phrase. Help them staple completed rocks to the board, letting the yellow "mortar" show in between. Challenge them to cover the board to make a rock wall.

Rock Centers

Language Center

Language Arts Standard
Identifies beginning sounds

Rocky Sounds

Materials
- activity master on page 50

Teacher Preparation: Duplicate the activity master for each child. Help children identify the pictures. Then challenge them to write the beginning letter or letters to complete the words.

Math Center

Math Standard
Compares and orders objects

Ordering Rocks

Materials
- 5 rocks in a variety of sizes
- balance scale
- permanent marker

Teacher Preparation: Without regard to size or shape, number the rocks in any order with the permanent marker.

Have children use the balance scale to determine the order of the rocks by weight. Next, have them order the rocks by size. They should record the order on paper using the numbers on the rocks.

Rock Centers

Science Center

Science Standard
Conducts simple descriptive investigations

Experiment with Rocks

Materials
- activity master on page 51
- limestone rocks
- water
- unbreakable jar with a lid

Teacher Preparation: Duplicate the activity master for each child.

Have children work in pairs to follow the experiment and record their observations.

Social Studies Center

Social Studies Standard
Identifies examples of and uses for natural resources

Rocks All Around

Materials
- activity master on page 52
- crayons

Teacher Preparation: Duplicate the activity master for each child.
Have children color all the rocks and things made of rocks.

Rock Centers

Writing Center

Language Standard
Writes in different forms for different purposes

Wishing on a Pebble

Materials
- *Sylvester and the Magic Pebble* by William Steig
- activity master on page 53

Teacher Preparation: Read *Sylvester and the Magic Pebble* to children. Duplicate the activity master for each child.

Invite children to make a list of three wishes that they would make if they had a magic pebble.

Communication Center

Science Standard
Observes and describes differences in rocks

Name That Rock

Materials
- resources about basic kinds of rocks
- rock field guides
- a variety of sedimentary, metamorphic, and igneous rocks
- hand lenses

Have partners observe and sort the rocks. Challenge children to guess which category each belongs to and discuss why they think as they do. Some students may enjoy identifying the name of each kind of rock by using the resources.

Rock Centers

Physical Development Skills Center

> **Physical Education Standard**
> Demonstrates a variety of relationships in dynamic movement situations such as behind, next to, left, and right

Stepping Stones

Materials
- pattern on page 54
- a blue sheet or large piece of blue felt
- tan or gray felt
- scissors

Teacher Preparation: Duplicate the pattern. Use it as a template to make about ten stepping stones. Cut out the shapes and lay them on the sheet or felt spread out on the floor.

Have children take turns giving and following directions as to where to move, such as left, right, backward, or forward. Suggest that children say or follow five directions before trading out.

Art Center

> **Art Standard**
> Expresses ideas through original artworks, using a variety of mediums

Be a Sculptor

Materials
- activity master on page 55
- resources that show stone sculptures
- clay
- craft sticks
- pencils

Teacher Preparation: Duplicate the activity master for each child. Then divide clay into three- or four-inch balls.

Display resources showing stone sculptures. Tell children that many famous sculptors will draw a design on paper first. Then they will make a clay model. Invite children to be a sculptor by drawing a design and using clay to make the form. Suggest that they can use a pencil and craft stick to add details.

Name _____ Date _____

Rhymes with *Rock*

Directions: Say each picture name. Write the letter or letters to complete the word.

Use with "Rocky Sounds" on page 46.

Name _____ Date _____

Do an Experiment

Directions: Get these things.

• soft rocks   • water   • a jar with a lid

Directions: Follow the steps.

1. Put the rocks carefully in a jar.
2. Add some water. Put on the lid tightly.
3. Shake the jar for a long time.
4. Look at the rocks.

Directions: Answer the question.

Did the rocks change? Tell what you see.

_____

_____

Use with "Experiment with Rocks" on page 47.

Name _____ Date _____

I See a Rock!

Directions: Color all the rocks and the things made of rocks.

Use with "Rocks All Around" on page 47.

Name _____ Date _____

Wish List

Directions: Imagine that you have a magic pebble. What three wishes would you make? Write them below.

1. _____
   _____
   _____

2. _____
   _____
   _____

3. _____
   _____
   _____

Use with "Wishing on a Pebble" on page 48.

Stone Pattern

Use with "Stepping Stones" on page 49.

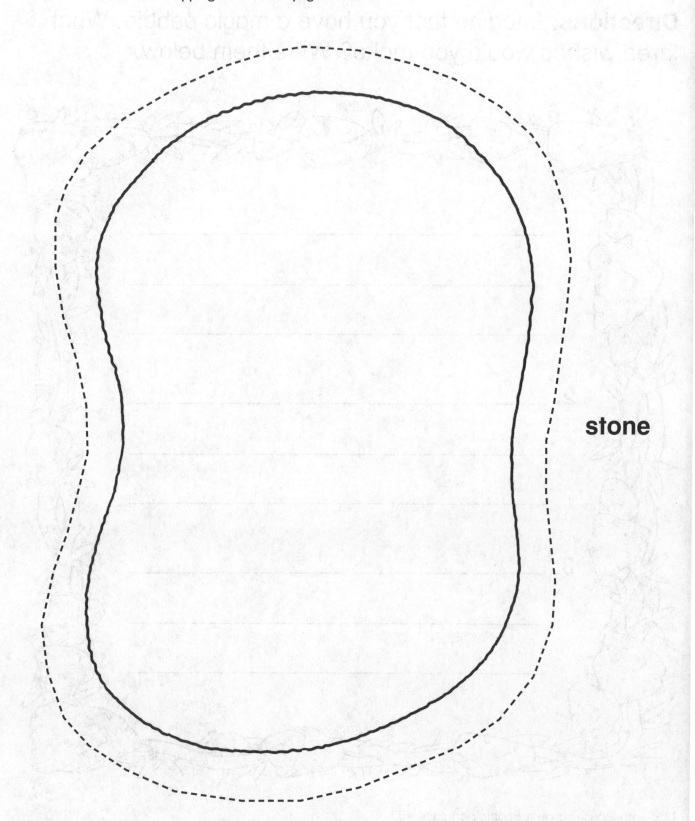

stone

Literature Selection: *Frog and Toad Are Friends* by Arnold Lobel

Ask children to discuss characteristics that make a good friend. List their responses on chart paper. Then read a chapter each day out of *Frog and Toad Are Friends*. Ask them to continue to think about words that describe a good friend after each chapter. Add the words to the chart. Afterward, have children complete the following activities.

Matching Buttons (for the chapter "A Lost Button")

Materials
- pattern on page 90
- a jar full of buttons
- glue or tape
- markers or crayons

Directions
Teacher Preparation: Duplicate, color, and cut out the pattern.

Invite children to choose three or four buttons that have one characteristic that is the same, such as color, number of holes, or size. Have them glue or tape the buttons on the coat. Then ask children to work with a partner to name the characteristic that is the same.

Letter to a Friend

Materials
- activity master on page 91

Directions
Teacher Preparation: Duplicate the activity master for each child.

Reread the letter that Frog writes to Toad. Lead children in a discussion of the details that Frog includes in the letter. Then ask why Frog would write a letter to a friend that he sees every day. Finally, invite children to write a letter on the activity master to a special friend. Be sure to review the correct letter format.

Books Authored and/or Illustrated by Arnold Lobel

- *The Book of Pigericks* (HarperCollins)
- *Days with Frog and Toad* (HarperCollins)
- *Dinosaur Time* (HarperTrophy)
- *Fables* (HarperCollins)
- *Frog and Toad All Year* (HarperCollins)
- *Frog and Toad Are Friends* (HarperCollins)
- *Frog and Toad Together* (HarperCollins)
- *How the Rooster Saved the Day* (Viking Children's Books)
- *Ming Lo Moves the Mountain* (Mulberry)
- *Mouse Soup* (HarperCollins)
- *Mouse Tales* (HarperCollins)
- *On Market Street* (HarperTrophy)
- *Owl at Home* (HarperCollins)
- *The Rose in My Garden* (Mulberry)
- *A Three Hat Day* (HarperTrophy)
- *A Treeful of Pigs* (Greenwillow)
- *Uncle Elephant* (HarperCollins)

Bookmark Patterns

Hop to it! Read a book about Frog and Toad!

Friends read books by Arnold Lobel.

Hats off to you . . . when you read A Three Hat Day!

Coat Pattern
Use with "Matching Buttons" on page 87.

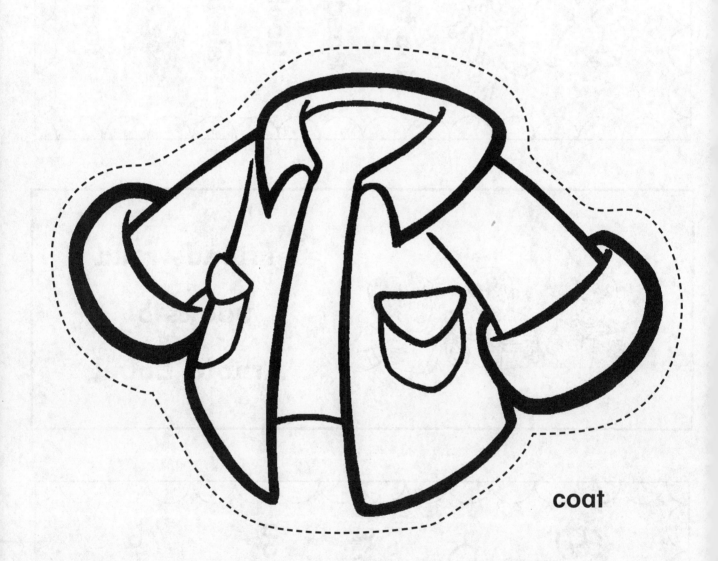

coat

Name _____ Date _____

Stationery

Directions: Write a letter to a special friend.

Dear _____,

_____

_____

_____

_____

_____

_____

_____

Your friend,

_____

Use with "Letter to a Friend" on page 87.

Center Icons Patterns

Art Center

Communication Center

Game Center

Language Center

Center Icons Patterns

Literacy Center

Math Center

Music Center

Physical Development Skills Center

Center Icons Patterns

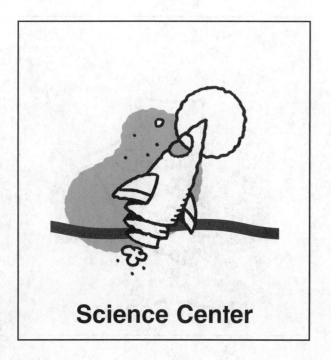

Science Center

Social Studies Center

Technology Center

Writing Center

Student Awards

Student Award

Let's celebrate!

_____
Child's name

can _____.

_____
Teacher's signature

_____
Date

Calendar Day Pattern

Suggested Uses
- Reproduce the card for each day of the month. Write the numerals on each card and place it on your class calendar. Use cards to mark special days.
- Reproduce to make cards to use in word ladders or word walls.
- Reproduce to make cards and write letters on each card. Children use the cards to play word games forming words.
- Reproduce to make cards to create matching or concentration games for children to use in activity centers. Choose from the following possible matching skills or create your own:
    — uppercase and lowercase letters
    — pictures of objects whose names rhyme, have the same beginning or ending sounds, or contain short or long vowels
    — pictures of adult animals and baby animals
    — number words and numerals
    — numerals and pictures of objects
    — colors and shapes
    — high-frequency sight words

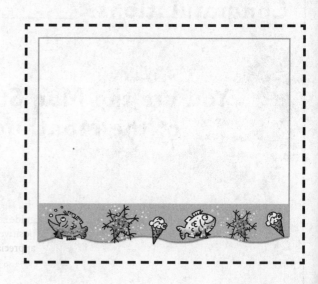